Month-by-Month
MASTERPIECES

Explorations of 10 Great Works with Step-by-Step Art Projects

by Bobbi Chertok, Goody Hirshfeld, and Marilyn Rosh

SCHOLASTIC
PROFESSIONAL BOOKS

New York • Toronto • London • Auckland • Sydney

Dedication

To Mark, Lauren, Rachel, Ari, Kaila, Morgan, Samantha, Jessica, Robert . . . and all the children of the next generation

Masterpiece Art Credits:

Allegory of California by Diego Rivera. Photo: Dirk Bakker, © The Detroit Institute of Arts, Fresco, Mexico City.

Autumn Rhythm by Jackson Pollock. The Metropolitan Museum of Art, George A. Hearn Fund, 1957 (57.92).

Bamboo in Wind and Rain by Tao-Chi. The Metropolitan Museum of Art, Edward Elliot Family Collection, Gift of Douglas Dillon, 1984 (1984.475.2).

Beasts of the Sea by Henri Matisse. National Gallery of Art, Washington, Alisa Mellon Bruce Fund.

Electrical Prisms by Sonia Delaunay. Musee National d'Art Moderne, Central National d'Art et de Culture Georges Pompidou.

Giant Hamburger by Claes Oldenburg. © Art Gallery of Ontario, Toronto, (66/29).

Holy Mountain III by Horace Pippin. Photo: Lee Stalsworth, © Hirshhorn Museum and Sculpture Garden, Smithsonian Institute, Gift of Joseph Hirshhorn, 1966. (66.4096).

Paris Through the Window by Marc Chagall. Photo: David Heald, © The Soloman R. Guggenheim Foundation, New York (FN 37.438).

Sky Cathedral by Louise Nevelson. Photo: © The Museum of Modern Art, Gift of Mr. and Mrs. Ben Mildwoff.

Starry Night by Vincent Van Gogh. Photo: © The Museum of Modern Art, acquired through the Lillie P. Bliss Bequest.

Interior design by Jaime Lucero and Robert Dominguez for Grafica, Inc.
Cover design by Vincent Ceci and Jaime Lucero
Illustrations by Mona Mark
Photo research by Daniella Jo Nilva

ISBN 0-590-25101-5

Printed in the U.S.A.

Acknowledgments

All the activities in this book were tested by an enthusiastic group of students and some very dedicated teachers. The authors wish to express their deepest appreciation to:

- **Sheila Estrin**, her third-grade class, and Peri Karkheck, the art teacher, at the Strawtown Road School in New City, New York
- **Eleanor Katz**, art teacher, and students at the Museum School, Yonkers, New York
- **Tom Muniz**, art teacher, and students at School 21, Yonkers, New York
- **Babs Reeder** and her third-grade class at Bardonia Elementary School, Bardonia, New York
- **Marlene Stifelman**, her second-grade class, and Josephine Carilli, the art teacher, at Congers Elementary School, Congers, New York

Our sincere thanks go to Al Loeb and Mel Rosh for photographing the students' work, and to Emily Roth, librarian, at the Metropolitan Museum of Art Library and Resource Center, for her kind assistance.

We extend our special appreciation to Liza Charlesworth for her ideas, insights, and enthusiastic support. And we are indeed grateful to Fran Weinberg, whose sensitive editing made this task a pleasure.

Table of Contents

About Living Arts Seminar

In 1973 Bobbi Chertok, Goody Hirshfeld, and Marilyn Rosh created Living Art Seminars, a nonprofit organization designed to bring fine art into the classroom through a variety of programs. Its goal is to make art fresh, fun, and relevant to each and every child. Thousands of elementary schoolchildren and their teachers have awakened to a new appreciation of art through Living Art Seminars. As part of this program, students and teachers also visit museums, where they discover the excitement and beauty of art. Students learn respect for and understanding of different cultures. The seminars stimulate critical thinking with emphasis on observing, sequencing, listening, and reasoning. As a writer for *The New York Times* has observed, "With the help of Living Art Seminars, students are discovering that art is a lot closer and more fun than they had imagined." Over the years, Living Art Seminars has received numerous state and local grants.

In 1992 the founders of Living Art Seminars captured some of their time-tested techniques in *Meet the Masterpieces: Strategies, Activities, and Posters to Explore Great Works of Art*. Published the following year, *Meet the Masterpieces: Learning About Ancient Civilizations Through Art* focused on eight ancient cultures. This third volume in the Masterpiece series highlights ten significant works of art, one for each of the ten months of the school year. All are published by Scholastic.

A Note to the Teacher

During each of the ten school months, you can introduce your class to a masterpiece created by a world-famous artist. These works will motivate your students to take a close look at art, to get excited enough to question what they see, and to create their own art-related projects (presented in detail in this book). By sharing these experiences, they will increase their understanding and appreciation of art. Best of all, since we have tested each of these projects in the classroom, we know you and your students will have fun while learning and working together.

The works of art appear in this book in the following order, and we've suggested a time slot for presenting each work to your class. However, you need not tie yourself to this arrangement and schedule. Work with the art in the order that makes the most sense to you, and that fits into your curriculum and school calendar.

SEPTEMBER	*Allegory of California* by Diego Rivera
OCTOBER	*Autumn Rhythm* by Jackson Pollock
NOVEMBER	*Sky Cathedral* by Louise Nevelson
DECEMBER	*Paris Through the Window* by Marc Chagall (sha-GAHL)
JANUARY	*Giant Hamburger* by Claes Oldenburg
FEBRUARY	*Holy Mountain III* by Horace Pippin
MARCH	*Starry Night* by Vincent Van Gogh (van-GO)
APRIL	*Bamboo in Wind and Rain* by Tao-Chi (DOW-chee)
MAY	*Electrical Prisms* by Sonia Delaunay (de-LAWN-ee)
JUNE	*Beasts of the Sea* by Henri Matisse (ON-ree mah-TEES)

The ten works of art discussed in the book are all masterpieces. Each is unique, and together they represent a range as diverse as art can be. Some, like Rivera's *Allegory of California* and Pippin's *Holy Mountain III*, show real objects that tell stories with important messages. Others, such as Chagall's *Paris Through the Window* and Matisse's *Beasts of the Sea*, transport us to magical worlds of make-believe. The works of Delaunay, Nevelson, and Pollock delight our senses with abstract shapes, colors, and textures; while the radiance of nature in the paintings of Van Gogh and Tao-Chi touches our spirits. With a completely different approach, Oldenburg's Pop Art makes us sit up and take notice. You will be bringing into your classroom ten extraordinary pieces of art. We invite you and your students to enjoy your visits with all of them.

How to Use This Book

Before You Begin

1. Relax. This is a book to enjoy. A prior knowledge of art is not necessary. If you can enjoy the art, you will motivate your students to react fully and freely to these works.

2. Some of the students' answers to the questions raised here may not be conventional, but diverse and divergent answers often lead to the most creative insights. For example, in discussing *Holy Mountain III*, we ask, "Why do you think Pippin placed children on his holy mountain?" Any answer connecting children to the painting is valid and deserves encouragement. Connections add to the richness and meaning of the discussion and enhance the appreciation of art. In defense of a variety of answers, we must remember that the artists who created these works broke rules themselves.

3. Preview each work of art before you introduce it. Read over the questions and possible answers. You need not ask all the questions, but may consider them mind joggers for yourself. Pick out the questions that seem relevant to your class, and feel free to add some of your own. Stay with the discussion as long as interest is high.

Getting Started

Each of the ten pieces of art occupies one section. Each section contains three parts:

• **Meet the Artist**   • **Close-up on the Art**   • **In the Style of the Artist**

9

Meet the Artist

This part has a brief biography of the artist. You may reproduce it and give it to students. It includes:

• A picture of the artist
• The artist's dates of birth and of death
• General background and interesting facts about the artist

The artists in this book come from seven different countries. One artist, Tao-Chi, was born over 300 years ago; while another, Claes Oldenburg, is creating art today. Many worked hard to overcome obstacles; but they all had one thing in common. Each artist struggled to find a boldly original way to create art; each one dared to be different.

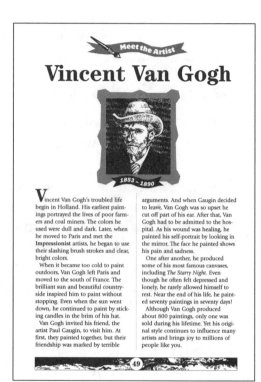

Meet the Artist

Vincent Van Gogh

1853 ~ 1890

Vincent Van Gogh's troubled life began in Holland. His earliest paintings portrayed the lives of poor farmers and coal miners. The colors he used were dull and dark. Later, when he moved to Paris and met the **Impressionist** artists, he began to use their slashing brush strokes and clear, bright colors.

When it became too cold to paint outdoors, Van Gogh left Paris and moved to the south of France. The brilliant sun and beautiful countryside inspired him to paint without stopping. Even when the sun went down, he continued to paint by sticking candles in the brim of his hat.

Van Gogh invited his friend, the artist Paul Gaugin, to visit him. At first, they painted together, but their friendship was marked by terrible

arguments. And when Gaugin decided to leave, Van Gogh was so upset he cut off part of his ear. After that, Van Gogh had to be admitted to the hospital. As his wound was healing, he painted his self-portrait by looking in the mirror. The face he painted shows his pain and sadness.

One after another, he produced some of his most famous canvases, including *The Starry Night*. Even though he often felt depressed and lonely, he rarely allowed himself to rest. Near the end of his life, he painted seventy paintings in seventy days!

Although Van Gogh produced about 800 paintings, only one was sold during his lifetime. Yet his original style continues to influence many artists and brings joy to millions of people like you.

49

Close-up on the Art

This part is the teacher's guide and the heart of the learning experience. The questions will encourage students to observe, react, imagine, and express their own feelings. Students' responses might lead to surprising and fascinating detours. To build your students' self-confidence in relating to art, try to encourage them to respond freely.

As you discuss each work, display the poster with the reproduction of the art in a prominent place in your classroom. For some posters, you might want to make a "frame" and hang it in an area where students can gather around it as in a museum.

Of the ten reproductions, only five feature oil paintings. The others show a mural, a hanging scroll, a collage, and two photographs of sculptures. It is important that students understand each medium is unique and how it differs from the others. The "Close-up" offers information about the various media. You might also give students an idea of the size of the original work of art, noted at the beginning of the "Close-up."

Close-up on the Art

THE STARRY NIGHT

ARTIST:
Vincent Van Gogh

SIZE:
2'5" x 3'

MEDIUM:
Oil on canvas

DATE:
1889

Most of us have had the experience of looking up in wonder at the night sky.

What moves in Vincent Van Gogh's sky?
Everything seems to be in motion. The rings that form halos around the moon and the stars seem to make them come alive. Paint forms great sweeping spirals of wind that swirl through the sky. They almost looks like waves rushing to the shore.

Which way is the wind moving? Let your hand describe the path of the wind.
Hand gestures can show rolling, swooping, spiraling motions.

What vertical objects did Van Gogh place in the landscape to keep our eyes from moving too quickly across the canvas?
The mysterious flame shape on the left is most probably one of the cypress trees that Van Gogh loved to paint. The church steeple also acts as a stop sign and keeps our eyes from rushing across the horizontal sky.

Where do you think the artist was standing when he saw this scene?
He was probably on a hill. Nobody is quite sure whether this painting represents an actual scene or is the result of Van Gogh's very active imagination. The village in the foreground may be one of the Dutch villages that Van Gogh remembered from his past.

50

In the Style of the Artist

This part enables your students to become artists. They work with the medium, the technique, and the style used by the artist they are studying.

This part has four subdivisions:

1. GOAL

States the aim of the art project.

2. WHAT YOU'LL NEED

Lists the materials needed for experimenting with/and completing the art project. Please feel free to substitute or add materials depending on individual needs and the availability of supplies. Crayons or markers can replace paint, staples or glue can substitute for needles and thread, and even small jewelry or shoe boxes can replace cartons if space is a problem.

When suggesting that you use paint or ink, we advise you to protect all surfaces with newspaper or drop cloths, and students' clothing with smocks or shirts. Plastic plates for mixing paints, and cups for washing brushes are important.

Above all, we encourage you to instruct students in the safe and proper handling of all tools; such as scissors, wire cutters, hole punchers, and so on.

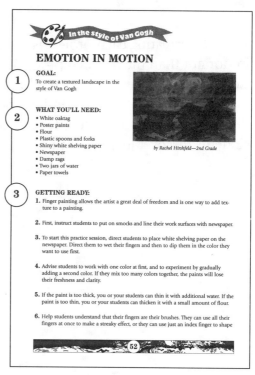

In the style of Van Gogh

EMOTION IN MOTION

① GOAL:
To create a textured landscape in the style of Van Gogh

② WHAT YOU'LL NEED:
- White oaktag
- Poster paints
- Flour
- Plastic spoons and forks
- Shiny white shelving paper
- Newspaper
- Damp rags
- Two jars of water
- Paper towels

by Rachel Hirshfeld—2nd Grade

③ GETTING READY:
1. Finger painting allows the artist a great deal of freedom and is one way to add texture to a painting.

2. First, instruct students to put on smocks and line their work surfaces with newspaper.

3. To start this practice session, direct students to place white shelving paper on the newspaper. Direct them to wet their fingers and then to dip them in the color they want to use first.

4. Advise students to work with one color at first, and to experiment by gradually adding a second color. If they mix too many colors together, the paints will lose their freshness and clarity.

5. If the paint is too thick, you or your students can thin it with additional water. If the paint is too thin, you or your students can thicken it with a small amount of flour.

6. Help students understand that their fingers are their brushes. They can use all their fingers at once to make a streaky effect, or they can use just an index finger to shape

52

3. GETTING READY

Gives students the opportunity to research or experiment before they begin the project itself. Like Diego Rivera, they will research and gather information about their community to plan a mural; like Jackson Pollock, they will experiment by dripping paint from a stick; like Sonia Delaunay, they will mix colors.

As you give students instructions, be clear about the safe and careful use of materials, but allow them freedom in trying different techniques.

4. LET'S BEGIN

Gives a step-by-step sequence for creating a work of art in the medium and style of a particular artist. Since the media and styles of these ten artists vary, your students will use different skills on each project. For example, they will create assemblages by stacking boxes, and make soft sculptures by sewing and stuffing fabric. Or they will use their fingers as brushes and draw with scissors. They will work cooperatively to make a mural and individually to design a scroll. They will create a fantasy and explore the technique of collage.

The act of creating each project is far more important than the finished product. Congratulate students for their efforts, and display their art for others to admire. And you deserve congratulations, too, for helping your students discover just how much fun art can be.

a more definite line. They can dab the paint on with knuckles or thumbs. Encourage students to invent different textures by using different parts of their hands.

7. Moving quickly, students might want to scrape various designs and textures into the paint with a plastic fork or spoon.

8. They should use the paper towels to blot any excess paint, and they should clean their fingers and tools with a damp rag when they change from one color to another.

9. When the students feel comfortable using finger paints, it is time to go on to the next step.

LET'S BEGIN:

1. Direct students to place fresh newspaper on their work surfaces and to put a piece of oaktag on top.

2. Suggest that students think of an outside scene—either a real or an imaginary landscape. What will the weather be? Is something moving through the air? Is it night or day? Are there mountains or valleys? Are there lakes or waterfalls?

3. Advise students that the sky is a good place to begin and that, like Van Gogh, they should let the sky take up at least half the painting. Encourage students to put some movement in the sky. Now is the time to dip fingers in a color and start.

4. Remind students not to mix together too many colors at once and to keep cleaning their hands with a damp rag.

5. By looking back at their experiments using plastic utensils or different parts of the hand, students can get ideas for adding some contrasting textures to their landscapes.

6. It is a good idea to allow the background sky to dry before students work on the foreground and the middle ground.

8. Van Gogh did not want to imitate nature. He experimented with color and rearranged and reshaped forms. Students too should let imagination and energy guide their hands as they move around the paper. Finally, encourage students to step back and admire the results of their flying fingers.

53

12

Diego Rivera

1886 - 1957

The Mexican artist Diego Rivera created hundreds of colorful murals, or wall paintings, that made history come alive.

By the age of ten, he had enrolled as the youngest student at the San Carlos Academy of Fine Arts in Mexico City. Later, he became fascinated with the culture of the early Mexican people, such as the Mayans and the Aztecs, who had created great art long before Columbus sailed to the "New World." Rivera's pride in his Mexican heritage lasted his whole life.

After studying modern art and ancient frescoes in Europe, Rivera returned to Mexico with a great purpose. He wished to paint not only for the wealthy few, but for *all* the people. They wouldn't have to buy his art. He would paint pictures for everyone to see—on huge walls in a clear style that was familiar to Mexicans. And he would paint the story of the Mexican people, their history, and their future.

Rivera's murals on public buildings in Mexico became very popular. People would flock to see the six-foot, 300-pound Rivera high up on scaffolding commanding a crew of artists and technicians. One of the admirers who came to watch was the artist Frida Kahlo. Soon after, Rivera and Kahlo were married.

They were invited to the United States where Rivera painted a mural for the Pacific Stock Exchange in San Francisco. He worked for months and months researching the subject of California. He made thousands of sketches before he began to paint. In his mural, the technology and inventions of the twentieth century show us a bright and promising future. Ordinary men and women appear with dignity and as heroes worthy of our respect.

ALLEGORY OF CALIFORNIA

ARTIST:
Diego Rivera

SIZE:
472 square feet

MEDIUM:
Fresco

DATE:
1931

Painting the truth as he saw it was always important to Diego Rivera. He used murals to express his beliefs.

What is a mural?

A mural is a wall painting. This particular kind of mural is a fresco, in which the paint has been applied directly to wet plaster. Since ancient times, artists have been painting palaces, churches, and public buildings with frescoes because they are a very permanent form of decoration.

Allegory of California rises high above the stairway of the City Club, next door to the Pacific Stock Exchange in San Francisco. It is the first mural that Rivera painted in the United States.

The mural is called *Allegory of California*. What is an allegory?

An allegory is a story or picture that uses characters and events to stand for abstract ideas. Often, an allegory teaches a moral lesson.

Can you guess which figure is supposed to represent the state of California?

Towering over the work is the super-sized figure of a woman. She represents the state of California embracing all its children as they benefit from the richness of the earth. Diego Rivera used the tennis player, Helen Wills Moody, as a model. He thought that her athletic beauty and strength were typical of the California woman.

What is around her neck?

She is wearing a golden necklace of wheat, one of the world's most important food crops.

What has she gathered up in her hands?

One hand clutches all the fruits of the earth while the other holds the precious minerals found under the ground.

How many different jobs can you find in the mural?

On the bottom left are the coal miners using modern machinery to drill a shaft. Above the miners is a lumberjack resting his hand on a redwood tree stump. To the left of the lumberjack are two figures: one an engineer, and the other a tool-maker or mechanic, both reading the blueprint on the table. At the bottom right are two miners panning for gold. The one standing is James Wilson Marshall, who made the first discovery of gold in California in 1848. The white-haired man kneeling above the miners is Luther Burbank, whose experiments improved the growing of fruits, trees, and other plants in California. A young man holding an airplane stands in the center of the mural. The airplane refers to the growth of the aviation industry, which was young at the time the mural was painted.

Can you guess why the young man has been placed in the middle of the mural?

He is the symbol of California's young people, whose intelligence and inventiveness will, according to Rivera, improve the future of the state. In addition to having the central position in the painting, the figure is bathed in bright sunlight.

What appears on either side of "California's" head?

To the left are oil rigs and an oil field. To the right are cargo ships, loading docks, derricks and cranes. All are symbols of California's industrial power.

Where did Rivera place the darkest colors in the mural?

The darkness of the underground coal mine gradually lightens as our eyes move upward to the sky.

MURAL, MURAL ON THE WALL

GOAL:

To create a mural of your state, community, or school in the style of Diego Rivera

WHAT YOU'LL NEED:

- Large roll of paper
- Crayons and/or markers
- Practice paper
- Masking tape

by Mrs. Estrin's 3rd Grade

GETTING READY:

1. Measure the wall or area you would like to use for your mural.

2. Cut an appropriate length of paper, and tape it on the wall.

3. Discuss with your class a theme for your mural. What makes your state, community, or school special? The mural can illustrate major activities that take place in your state; the variety of its citizens, its resources or strengths, its history, its famous people, past and present. Or do something similar for your community or school.

4. Help the class work together to plan characters, settings, and events for the mural. What will be the central figure? You might want to think of the most important people, sites, and events in your state, community, or school. Like Rivera, you might want to take the time to do some research.

5. Perhaps you will want to divide the class into small groups, each responsible for painting a particular section of the mural. Like Rivera, your students should make sketches on practice paper before beginning to paint.

6. Guide the class to decide on a background color that will help unify all the sections of the mural.

LET'S BEGIN:

1. Advise students to put in the large, bold shapes first. Remind them that bright colors are easier to see than subtle or murky colors.

2. Explain that figures on the mural must be large enough for viewers to see from a distance. Diego Rivera greatly enlarged the woman who represents California. Your students may choose to exaggerate the size of certain objects or people too.

3. Show students the benefit of stepping away from the mural as they are working.

4. Encourage classmates to consult with each other if they have a problem deciding on the color or placement of an object or figure.

5. Congratulations! You are in good company. Like Diego Rivera, Leonardo da Vinci, and Michelangelo, you and your class have created a mural.

Jackson Pollock

1912 ~ 1956

Jackson Pollock was born on a farm in Cody, Wyoming. He was a moody teenager, and the only classes he enjoyed in high school were painting and clay modeling.

During the summer, he worked with his father surveying land in Arizona and California. He would watch Native Americans making sand paintings by trickling or dripping colored sand. He developed a deep respect for Native American culture. Later, he would use sand-painting in his art.

By 1930 Jackson Pollock had moved to New York City. There, many young artists and writers met in cafés to share ideas about new ways to paint. Pollock was fascinated with the idea that an artist could express his innermost thoughts. He remembered the sand paintings he had seen in the past. Why couldn't he express his own feelings by dripping paint?

In 1947 Pollock began tacking his canvases to the floor and he dripped, splattered, and swirled paint on top. Pollock said he really got "in" the painting. His method was later called Action Painting.

Pollock had created a new style of art. It is totally abstract; meaning it does not picture people or places. It is an expression of his deepest feelings. Art critics named it Abstract Expressionism.

On August 11, 1956, Pollock lost control of his car at a bend in the road. He died instantly at the age of forty-four. Pollock's bold art greatly influenced a new group of artists who flocked to New York, making the United States the center of the art world.

AUTUMN RHYTHM

ARTIST:
Jackson Pollock

SIZE:
8′9″ x 17′3″

MEDIUM:
Oil on canvas

DATE:
1950

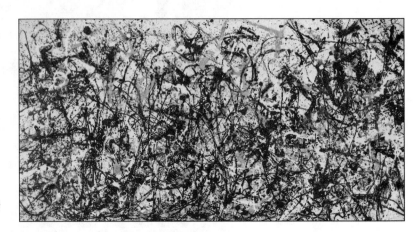

A line can form a shape you can recognize. It can curve around and become the outline of a bird or an elephant. But sometimes a line is wonderful just for its own sake.

Pick a line from the painting *Autumn Rhythm*. Is it possible to follow it as it winds its way in and out and up and down through the picture?

Most of the lines are so long and twisting that it is hard to discover where they begin and where they end. Just when you think you know where the line is going, it surprises you and hides behind another line or takes off in a completely different direction. Following the lines makes us active participants in this painting.

Do you think Jackson Pollock painted this web of lines with a brush?

He placed his canvas, the material on which an artist paints, on the floor. He walked or crawled on the canvas as he dribbled paint from a stick or poured it from a can. Some of his lines would end up thick. Others would be thin. Walking on his painting made Pollock feel as if he were actually "in" his painting. As he dripped and poured, he moved his arms in great big swirls and turned his body from side to side with enormous energy and purpose.

Can you guess why this style of art was called Action Painting?

The artist was actively moving while making the painting.

Do you think that Pollock could predict how each line would look before he dripped it on his painting?

Pollock didn't plan his paintings before he started, but once he began his feelings would explode onto the canvas. Sometimes the path a line would take was accidental. Sometimes Pollock would carefully control where he placed his lines so that the painting would have balance.

Why didn't Jackson Pollock paint familiar objects?

There are no familiar objects in this great mass of overlapping lines. Pollock was able to paint his feelings without including recognizable objects. He allowed his emotions to guide his hands and arms as he worked. A painting that has no recognizable objects is called abstract. An abstract painting that shows feelings is called Abstract Expressionism.

Why do you think this painting is titled *Autumn Rhythm*?

The colors Pollock chose are the colors of that time of year when winter will soon come. Rhythm in a painting refers to lines or repeated shapes that make our eyes flow over the surface of the painting. Pollock did not make one part of his painting more important than another, and so we keep moving through the painting, rhythmically, without stops and starts.

Would the painting be as exciting if Pollock had used all dark colors? Can you find the bright white lines that add contrast?

If Pollock had used all dark colors, we could not follow the intertwining lines, and the painting would seem to have very little movement.

How might the size of the original painting affect the viewer?

Autumn Rhythm is a huge painting—8 feet 9 inches by 17 feet 3 inches. Measure this area on a classroom wall to show how much space it occupies. When you are standing close to a painting this large, it seems to put you inside a whole new environment.

ACTION JACKSON

GOAL:
To create a drip painting in the style of Jackson Pollock

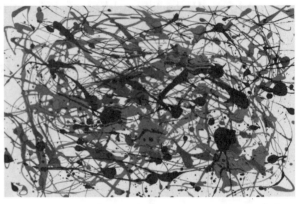

WHAT YOU'LL NEED:
This project will need some advance preparation. Students should begin collecting objects that can be used to drip, fleck, or splatter paint. Such objects include:

- Plastic squeeze bottles
- Tongue depressors
- String
- Toothbrushes

by Jose Tejada—4th Grade

In addition, you will need:
- Newspaper to protect the desk and floor
- Practice paper
- Manila or heavy white paper (11" x 18")
- Jars of poster paint
- Masking tape

GETTING READY:
Jackson Pollock felt he could best express his feelings by painting his action picture on a canvas laid flat on the floor.

1. You can choose to let students work on the floor or on top of their desks. In any case, protect their work surface by covering it with plenty of newspapers. Protect clothes by asking students to wear smocks or oversize shirts.

2. Next, you might want students to tape practice paper to the newspaper. If they are working on the floor, make sure they leave enough room to walk around the perimeter of their "canvas."

3. Ask students to select a color and stir that paint with a tongue depressor. If it seems too thick to drip, advise them to thin it with a little water.

4. Now students can try out some of the tools they have collected. Invite them to compare the different textures that result from dripping paint from a tongue depressor to pulling string along a paper's surface. How does paint splatter when it is flicked from the bristles of a toothbrush or squeezed from a plastic bottle? Which tools will produce a thin line? Which will produce a thick line? Remember, this can be messy—so take care!

5. Encourage students to experiment by varying their hand gestures. What kind of drips do they get when they move their hands rapidly? How does the line change when they move slowly?

LET'S BEGIN:

1. Jackson Pollock chose autumn as his theme. Ask students to choose their favorite time of year. Ask them to consider why they prefer this particular season.

2. Direct each student to select three colors. One color should be dark, another light, and the third a medium tone.

3. Ask students to secure their Manila paper to well-protected areas on the floor or desk.

4. Tell students to begin by selecting one of the three colors to start dripping. They might begin by making the lines long, flowing, and continuous. They can then vary their hand gestures. After a while, ask them to move on to the two other colors.

5. Remind students to feel free to substitute different tools at any time.

6. Results may be totally unexpected. It is almost impossible to completely plan a painting of this kind, so students must just let the painting happen. They will probably have many "fortunate accidents."

7. It is hard to know when to stop painting. There is always the danger of overworking a painting. When a student feels a painting is finished, encourage him or her to put away materials so as not to be tempted to put in just one more line. Make room available for their paintings to dry.

8. Work with students to create appropriate titles for their paintings. This is a good opportunity for brainstorming individually or in groups. Lastly, congratulate yourselves on a successful effort!

Louise Nevelson

1899 – 1988

Louise Nevelson knew she wanted to be a sculptor when she was only nine years old. But she had to wait forty-nine years before she was recognized as an important artist. During all this time, she never gave up her dreams. Even when she was living alone in poverty because no one wanted to exhibit or buy her work, she still believed in herself.

She was born in 1899 in Kiev, Russia. In 1905, her family immigrated to the United States to begin new lives in the seaport town of Rockland, Maine. When she was six years old, Nevelson had to learn a new language and start school in a strange environment.

Because she was a child in a new country, she always felt out of place. However, she was secure with crayons or watercolors in her hands. Art became her escape from every difficulty in her life.

At the age of twenty, Nevelson left Maine to study with some of the most talented artists of the time. She had a way of attracting interesting people. Once she helped Diego Rivera on a mural, and many famous artists, writers, and musicians became her lifelong friends.

People were fascinated by Nevelson's unconventional appearance. She wore long, black mink eyelashes, dramatic clothing, and fantastic hats, and even smoked long, thin cigars.

She loved to break tradition, and was daring not only in her style of dress. Her sculpture is unlike any other—huge assemblages of wooden boxes stacked one upon the other had never before been seen in the art world.

Although it took Nevelson a long time to achieve fame, today her original and unique art is displayed both inside and outside office buildings and major museums all over the world.

SKY CATHEDRAL

ARTIST:
Louise Nevelson

SIZE:
11'3" x 10' x 1'6"

MEDIUM:
Painted wood

DATE:
1958

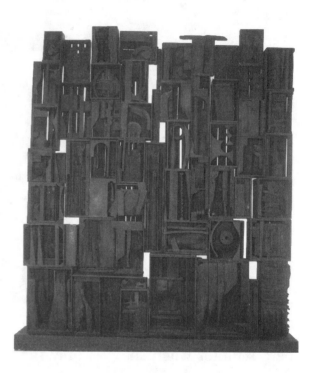

Louise Nevelson once said, "I love to put things together." In *Sky Cathedral*, she has put together about sixty boxes of different sizes. Louise Nevelson's assemblage reaches a height of eleven feet and is ten feet long.

Why did Louise Nevelson make this sculpture so large?

A person standing in front of this work feels surrounded by an unknown and strange environment. A smaller wall sculpture would not have as much power.

Can you guess what the strange bits and pieces of wood inside the boxes stand for or mean?

Although we may not understand or recognize these objects, they were all important to the artist. The boxes that she piled one on top of another are almost like secret hiding places. In them, she enclosed objects that appealed to her. Some of these objects have private meanings that only the artist could explain. Some individual boxes have doors that make us wonder what they are concealing. In many ways, this sculpture is a diary that uses wooden objects instead of words.

Are any of these shapes supposed to remind us of things we might see in the real world?

There seem to be some recognizable objects, such as chair legs, door knobs, and handles. However, most are mysterious constructions of found objects. These objects lose their familiarity when viewed in this context. Then the entire sculpture becomes an assemblage of abstract shapes that no longer refer to any particular person, place, or thing.

Which geometric shape is repeated the most often?

The object-filled boxes are all rectangles. The entire sculpture forms one large, slightly uneven rectangle.

Can you find any other repeated shapes?

Circles, half moons, and arcs contrast with the many straight lines.

How is this sculpture different from most other sculptures?

Unlike most sculptures that are meant to be walked around and viewed from all sides, Sky Cathedral was designed to go against the wall with the boxes facing outward.

How does the solid color affect you?

Both the inside and the outside are painted black, a color the artist loved. Using one color unifies all the separate parts and makes them add up to one whole. Nevelson once had her entire apartment painted black because she felt black created the most comfortable environment.

Did you notice the openings, or holes, in the sculpture?

They, too, are part of the design. To understand how important an opening can be, think of a donut. The edible part of the donut occupies the positive space. Both the hole and the space around the donut are the negative space. Both positive and negative space are necessary to the design.

Can you guess why Nevelson called this sculpture *Sky Cathedral*?

A cathedral is a large church. Its spires usually draw the viewer's eyes upward. Like a cathedral, Nevelson's sculpture also begins with the larger shapes on the bottom; the shapes gradually get smaller and smaller as they move toward the top.

If you could retitle this work, what words would you use to name the sculpture?

This is an opportunity for brainstorming and/or clustering. Words that may occur to students include hard, straight, curved, angular, massive, puzzle, hide-and-seek.

A WALL SCULPTURE

GOAL:

To create individual boxes that will be assembled into a wall sculpture in the style of Louise Nevelson

WHAT YOU'LL NEED:

This project will require some advance preparation. Each student should bring to class:

by Mrs. Estrin's 3rd Grade

- A sturdy box of any size—perhaps, a shoe box or medium-size carton
- An assortment of objects that will be used to decorate the inside of the box

The objects selected should reflect the interests and taste of the individual student. They may include:

- Molded Styrofoam
- Egg cartons
- Molded packaging
- Pieces of broken toys

- Cylindrical oatmeal boxes
- Tubes from paper towels, etc.
- Pieces of old jigsaw puzzles
- Wooden wheels, buttons, etc.

Note:

1. Please, no glass or objects with sharp edges.
2. These objects will not be returned. They will be painted and become a permanent part of the sculpture.

OTHER MATERIALS:

- Poster paint
- Masking tape
- Stapler

- Large brushes
- Brass fasteners
- Heavy paper

- Bottles of white glue
- Cord
- Glue gun*

- Wire
- Wire cutters
- Scissors

* Parents and other adults can help in this project, especially in assembling the sculpture and when using the glue gun.

GETTING READY:

Louise Nevelson thought of each box that went into her large constructions as an individual piece of art.

1. Each student needs a large enough work surface to hold his or her box and collected materials.

2. The front of each box should be open. Help students cut off any extra cardboard flaps from the front of the carton.

3. Give students time to arrange and rearrange their personal objects inside the boxes. Students can temporarily fasten objects to the inside surfaces with masking tape.

4. If students do not like the placement of an object, encourage them to pull off the tape and try again.

5. Show how an object will look different if turned upside-down, sideways, or even inside-out. Suggest that students hide a special object under or behind something else.

6. Students can also follow the directions below to make three-dimensional shapes out of heavy paper. These shapes create positive and negative space inside the boxes, adding variety and interest.

   - **Spiral:** Cut out a circle. Beginning on the perimeter, cut round and round, making smaller and smaller circles.
   - **Cylinder:** Cut out a rectangle. Roll it up, and fasten the edges with tape.
   - **Cone:** Cut out a circle. Make another cut from the edge to the center of the circle. Overlap the two straight edges you have created. Fasten with tape.
   - **Accordion Fold:** Cut out a rectangle, and fold it into narrow strips by bending the paper back and forth on itself.

LET'S BEGIN:

1. Now that your students know where they intend to place their collected and cut-out objects, they can start affixing them permanently.

2. Some objects will be easy to paste with white glue. Others will require masking tape or a stapler. Remember, tape will not show because the entire box will be painted.

3. Remind students not to paste any objects on outside surfaces of the boxes.

4. Each time a student pastes something within a box, he or she should step back and see if its placement works. Is the box balanced? Does it appear heavier on one side than on the other?

5. Once they have finished pasting, it is time for the entire class to select a color. Although the students began by working separately, all their boxes will become part of one large sculpture. Therefore, all students must paint their boxes the same color.

6. When the class has agreed upon the color, students should cover their work surfaces with newspapers and put on their smocks. It is best to mix the paint with some white glue to help the paint stick to any shiny or paint-resistant surfaces. Each student will paint his or her own box—every surface except the back of the box.

7. When the boxes are dry, it is time for you and your students to assemble the sculpture. Place the larger boxes on the bottom to prevent the sculpture from tipping over. As in *Sky Cathedral*, thrust some boxes forward; set others back.

8. Begin stacking all the boxes horizontally and vertically. The class might want to make the top of the sculpture irregular. As you assemble your sculpture, step back with the students to see if the arrangement is pleasing and balanced.

9. The class can join the boxes together using one of two methods, both of which require help from adults: (A) A glue gun is the better method, but hot glue can burn. (B) The other method needs the help of adults to punch holes in the cartons and then to secure the boxes to one another with string or wire.

10. When you are finished, decide with students on a good title for your sculptured wall. Take time to shake hands all around and to congratulate yourselves on a wonderful team effort.

Marc Chagall

1887 - 1985

Marc Chagall was born into a poor but lively Jewish family and grew up in the Russian village of Vitebsk (VEE-tepsk).

Instead of paying attention in school, he spent hours daydreaming. He imagined the animals and characters in the Bible stories he loved. Soon, only drawing and painting held his attention.

When he was twenty-three, Chagall received a small scholarship to study art in Paris, where he learned many new techniques and styles. But he always returned to memories of Vitebsk. Thousands of miles from home, Chagall gave life to his dreams. In bright, sweet, and tender paintings, his uncle fiddled on a rooftop, goats and cows smiled, tailors sewed, and peasants danced.

Chagall returned to Russia in 1914 and had to stay there because World War I had begun. He married the love of his life, Bella. The happy couple moved to Moscow, and Chagall began to paint huge scenery for the Jewish Art Theater, where Bella was an actress.

By 1922, the Chagalls had returned to Paris, but during the persecution of Jews in World War II, Chagall and his family had to escape from Europe and flee to the United States. When Bella died in 1944, Chagall could no longer dream. For almost a year, he did not pick up his paintbrush.

In the 1950's, Chagall returned to France, remarried, and once again, blossomed as an artist. He created magnificent mosaics and stained-glass windows for churches, synagogues, and buildings such as the Metropolitan Opera House in New York City. Until his death at ninety-seven, Chagall continued to share the private world of his imagination with art lovers everywhere.

PARIS THROUGH THE WINDOW

ARTIST:
Marc Chagall

SIZE:
4′5 1/2″ x 4′7 3/4″

MEDIUM:
Oil on canvas

DATE:
1913

Chagall often painted his memories and his dreams. In a dream some things may seem real, while others may not. In the painting *Paris Through the Window*, Chagall combines his inner world of memories and the outer world of reality.

Which objects in the painting seem magical or made-up?

In Chagall's magical dream world; a cat can be green and yellow and have a human face, a train can travel upside-down through the sky, two people can fly head to head, a person can float down to earth on a handkerchief-sized parachute, and a two-headed man can have a blue face.

Can you guess who the two-headed man might be? Could it be Chagall? If so, why is he facing in two directions?

It is possible that he is looking back to his past as well as looking forward to the future.

Can you find something in the painting that might be a memory from Chagall's past?

The man and woman flying sideways through the sky are dressed as townspeople from Vitebsk, the Russian village of his birth.

Can you find an object that reminds us of Chagall's new life in France?

The Eiffel Tower once rose higher than any other structure in the world. To Chagall, it probably represented the marvels of the modern world.

Why do you think Chagall painted images of both the past and the present in the same painting?

Chagall was not interested in painting only the real world. In his dream world, he could transport objects through time and space. Townspeople from the village he lived in when he was a young man could exist alongside scenes of modern Paris.

Many of Chagall's paintings celebrate love. Can you find two symbols, or signs, of love in this painting?

Chagall placed both symbols of love inside the house. He often used a bouquet of flowers as a declaration of love. A heart decorates the two-headed man's hand. Chagall's painted world is rarely scary or angry. More often, it is filled with love, hope, and good humor.

Is this an inside or an outside picture?

It is both. The man, chair, and flowers are inside the room. The cat is on the windowsill. Everything else is outside the window.

Why do you think Chagall put this cat in the painting?

Like the Egyptian Sphinx (which we associate with a riddle or a puzzle), the cat has the head of a human and the body of an animal. Chagall believed that since many things in life are puzzles that cannot be explained, we must have faith. Often his paintings are like fairy tales. If Little Red Riding Hood could talk to a wolf, and the Three Little Pigs could build houses, then why couldn't an animal have a human head?

Chagall's paintings often contain the colors of the rainbow, which are red, orange, yellow, green, blue, indigo, and violet. How many colors of the rainbow do you see in this painting?

They are all in this painting. These brilliant colors and the white background add to the lighthearted feeling of the picture.

This painting includes many repeated geometric shapes. How many triangles can you identify?

There are several, including the one that contains the artist's signature and the one that begins at the man's chin and goes past the cat's head.

What other shapes can you find?

The richly colored window frame is a group of squares. Their shape is repeated in the windows of the upside-down train. The buildings of Paris are also a jumble of geometric shapes. These shapes are all as important to the design of the painting as the floating figures and the Eiffel Tower.

JUST IMAGINE!

GOAL:

To create a fantasy picture in the style of Chagall

WHAT YOU'LL NEED:

In this activity, choose paint, crayon, or markers for coloring the final pictures.

by Alexandra Bartolotta—3rd Grade

- Several sheets of practice paper
- Crayons or markers
- Poster paints (optional)
- Brushes (optional)
- Newspaper
- Heavy white paper
- Jars of water (optional)
- Glue
- Scissors
- Plastic plates to mix colors (optional)

GETTING READY:

1. Invite your students to think of themselves inside a familiar room. It can be a room at school or at home.

2. Ask students to think of the objects they would ordinarily find in their familiar place. Then ask them to take a practice paper and to make a quick sketch of the room as they remember it.

3. Suggest that they draw the large shapes first. If, for example, a student is drawing the kitchen, he or she might want to begin with the large shape of the table, the refrigerator, or the stove.

4. Point out that Chagall used a window to open his painting to the outside. Perhaps your students, too, might want to fit a window into their compositions.

5. When students are satisfied with their sketches, they are ready to go on to the next step. This is the time for them to exercise their imagination and enter a world of fantasy, like Chagall's.

6. Ask, "What would be the most unexpected, strange, or magical object that could appear in your room?" You might suggest a red and purple unicorn, lollipops floating just below the ceiling, or an upside-down rosebush outside the window. Remind students about Chagall's imaginative self-portrait in *Paris Through the Window*. They, too, might want to include self-portraits.

7. Ask them to sketch each fantastic object or figure as it occurs to them. Students should use a separate piece of paper for this step.

8. Next, tell students to cut out their pictures of the unexpected and place the cut-out pieces of paper on the sketches of their rooms. Students should move the cutouts around until pleased with their positions.

9. Repeat that the pictures are not meant to mirror the real world. Objects can look like they're floating or flying. People can be blue, green, or two-headed.

10. Students should feel free to make changes. Perhaps they would like to increase the size of some objects or make others smaller. When students are entirely pleased with their compositions, they should glue down the cut-out papers.

11. Direct students to use crayons to color in the sketches. This exercise will help them decide which colors to use in their final versions. They might want to choose the rainbow colors that Chagall loved.

LET'S BEGIN:

1. Ask students to begin by covering the work space with newspaper, over which they will place a large piece of white paper. They are now ready to begin the final version of their fantasy pictures.

2. Using their practice papers as guides, students will copy their original sketch plus the fantasy elements onto the fresh paper.

3. If students are using crayons or markers, now is the time to color their fantasy pictures. If students are using paint, they can mix colors in the plastic plates. Like Chagall, they may want to lighten colors by mixing in white. Caution students to rinse brushes before going from one color to the next.

4. Remind students to sign and title their pictures when they are finished.

Claes Oldenburg

1929 -

Claes Oldenburg was born in Stockholm, Sweden. When he was a child, his family moved to Chicago. His first job was as a newspaper reporter, but he soon realized that instead of writing about events, he wanted to create them. His love of art gave him that opportunity.

In 1960, Oldenburg drove down a street in New York City and noticed many shops packed with merchandise. Suddenly, he saw the stores as museums and the colorful items on display as important as paintings.

As a result, Oldenburg began sewing and stuffing a sculpture in the shape of a sneaker. He did not intend this sneaker to be worn. Instead, for the first time, an everyday sneaker was to be looked upon as a work of art.

Oldenburg became the shopkeeper and sold his soft sculptures in a place he called The Store. At The Store, he began to act out events called happenings. He put people, objects, sounds and music together with his sculptures and watched what happened. He wanted to see how the people reacted.

When he moved to a much bigger store, his soft sculpture became giant-sized. He began creating fantasy hamburgers and furry Good Humor bars, which made adults smile and feel very young indeed. He invited artists and writers to parties where all the food looked good enough to eat but, in fact, was art.

By making typewriters and telephones soft and by making other small objects-like spoons and clothespins-enormous, Oldenburg forces us to look at our world in new ways. He startles us so much that we ask the question, "How important are all the everyday objects in our lives?"

GIANT HAMBURGER

ARTIST:
Claes Oldenburg

SIZE:
4 1/2' x 7'

MEDIUM:
Fabric, foam rubber,
and paint

DATE:
1962

Claes Oldenburg's experiments with soft sculptures have changed ideas of what sculpture can look like.

If you could touch Oldenburg's hamburger, how do you think it would feel?

This sculpture does not use traditional hard materials such as marble, bronze, and stone. Instead, the hamburger shape was cut out of a heavy fabric called sailcloth, sewn together, and painted. Like a bed pillow, it was then stuffed with foam rubber. However, you probably would not want to rest your head upon its surface. Painted fabric can be scratchy and hard.

How big do you think the hamburger sculpture is?

It's almost four and a half feet high, probably as tall as many children in elementary grades. It is seven feet in diameter, as long as a basketball player lying on the floor.

Why do you think the artist made this sculpture so large?

If it were the size of an ordinary hamburger, people probably would not pay much attention to it. A hamburger is so common, so familiar to the American lifestyle, that we take its form and shape for granted. But when an everyday object like a hamburger becomes super-sized, it surprises us into seeing it with new eyes. We now approach the hamburger with an open mind. The ordinary has become extraordinary art.

Why is a giant hamburger an appropriate symbol of life in the United States today?

The hamburger is the most popular and visible fast food in the United States today. McDonald's golden arches are recognizable to almost every child and adult. People can get in their car, drive down the highway, pull up to the drive-in window, and buy a ready-made hamburger. Most burgers look alike; the meat is shaped into a round patty and fits comfortably in a round roll. Sometimes it is garnished with lettuce, a pickle, or ketchup, but its basic shape seldom varies. It is a product of the United States' industrial society. It is eaten by young and old, rich and poor. It can be ordered in fancy restaurants or served at backyard barbecues. It can be prepared very quickly and eaten just as fast. In many ways, it reflects a way of life in the United States.

Oldenburg is called a Pop Artist. Can you guess how Pop Art got its name?

Pop probably comes from the word popular. Pop Art explores the reality of everyday life. It pays particular attention to mass-produced objects. Its designs are usually dramatic and suggest a sense of fun.

SEW BIG

by Stephanie Leibert—6th Grade

GOAL:

To create a soft sculpture in the style of Claes Oldenburg

WHAT YOU'LL NEED:

In this project, students can sew, staple, or glue the fabric. A search through a closet or junk drawer may turn up interesting bits of yarn, fabric, or cord.

- Scissors
- Glue or stapler
- Fabrics (panty hose, cotton, felt, etc.)
- Thread
- Stuffing material
  (newspaper, fiberfill, feathers, shredded foam, old rags, etc.)

- Needles with large eyes
- Colored yarns
- Straight pins with plastic heads
- Newspaper (for a pattern)

GETTING READY:

1. Ask students to choose a simple item or package of food or drink that appeals to them. It can be a carrot, a chocolate-chip cookie, a cereal box, or any other common edible object, or wrapping for such an object.

The following directions will use a carrot as an example. Your students, of course, will make patterns appropriate to the items they have selected.

2. Ask students to think about the shapes of the items they have chosen. The carrot, for example, has a long, narrow triangular shape; a chocolate-chip cookie is round; a cereal box is rectangular; and so on.

3. To make a pattern for a carrot sculpture, a student would have to draw a triangle on a large piece of newspaper and cut it out. If the triangle is not long or wide enough, the student should try again.

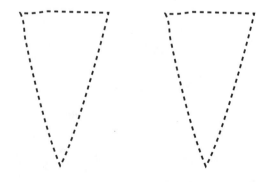

4. When students have created a workable pattern, explain that they will need to make a copy of it so that they will have two patterns.

LET'S BEGIN:

1. Students now select an appropriate fabric for their individual sculptures. They may need to trade materials they've brought from home. Like Oldenburg, who paints his sculptures, students may paint fabric if they cannot find fabric in the color they consider appropriate for their soft sculptures.

2. Carefully using straight pins, students will pin each of the two paper patterns to pieces of fabric and cut out the fabric. Each student will wind up with two pieces for his or her sculpture (or more if creating a sculpture with more than one part).

3. If students have selected an object, such as a cereal box, that requires writing or illustrations, now, while it is flat, is the time to paint or draw on the fabric. Students might want to sketch the words or designs in pencil and then use paint, marker, or crayon to color them. Advise students to wait for paint to dry before proceeding.

4. Students are now ready to sew, glue, or staple the seams of the sculptures. Explain that the wrong side of their fabric should face outward. Then the students can begin to stitch, glue, or staple the two pieces on all but one side. No matter what the shape of the pattern they are working with, students must leave an opening wide enough to accommodate the stuffing and a child's fingers or hand. For example, if a student is making a soft sculpture of a carrot, he or she should not sew the tops of the triangles. The top must remain open so that the student can stuff the carrot.

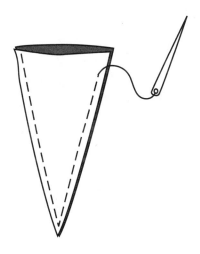

5. When finished with joining all but one side, students can turn the fabric inside out so that the right side is visible.

6. As students stuff their sculptures, encourage them to distribute the stuffing evenly throughout.

7. Then, tell students to sew, glue, or staple the opening.

8. To complete their soft sculptures, students might need other finishing touches or additional details. A soft-sculpture carrot, for example, needs lacy leaves and a stem. Ask students what they would use to make the chocolate chips on a soft-sculpture cookie. The choice of materials is up to the students. They can paint, paste, or add yarn or wire as needed.

9. The class might want to arrange all the finished sculptures on a table or design a Pop Art supermarket stocked with soft-sculpture items.

Horace Pippin

1888 - 1946

When he was a child growing up in West Chester, Pennsylvania, Horace Pippin loved to draw. At fourteen, Pippin left school to help support his family. He worked as a stable boy on a farm and as a hotel porter. He had no spare time to paint.

When the United States entered World War I, Pippin wanted to help fight for his country. He entered the 369th Regiment, which was the first unit of African-American soldiers to go overseas. Pippin recorded his terrible experiences in words and pictures.

When Pippin was wounded in action, a steel plate was inserted in his right shoulder and remained there for the rest of his life. His right arm became shriveled. For eleven years after he returned home, Pippin couldn't draw.

One day he noticed a poker next to a potbellied stove. He found a piece of wood, and supporting his weak right hand with his left, he began to burn a picture into the wood with the poker. It took a year for him to finish the burnt wood panel. Once again, he was an artist.

Horace Pippin painted his painful memories of the war. It was his way of healing his spirit, which, like his arm, had been wounded by the war. He also painted memories of his childhood. He once said, "Pictures just come to my mind and then I tell my heart to go ahead."

Pippin was the first self-taught African-American artist to gain recognition for his paintings. In the fifty years since his death, his paintings have been exhibited in major museums throughout the United States and the rest of the world.

HOLY MOUNTAIN III

> **ARTIST:**
> Horace Pippin
>
> **SIZE:**
> 2'1" x 2'6 1/4"
>
> **MEDIUM:**
> Oil on fabric
>
> **DATE:**
> 1945

Horace Pippin was very familiar with a biblical passage that predicted a time of peace in the world. The passage says that a wolf shall lie down with a lamb and a child shall lead us all. The Old Testament also says, "They shall not hurt nor destroy in all my holy mountain" (Isaiah XI:9). Pippin completed two other Holy Mountain paintings. In each, the message was the same.

Can you find the holy mountain in this painting?

When you are on top of a mountain, you do not necessarily see its shape and form. The bright green expanse of grass probably represents the mountain plateau—a comfortable, serene environment where special things can happen.

In this painting, how did Pippin illustrate his ideas about peace?

A lamb, a lion, and a wolf sit in the grass without fear of one another. There is a stillness about all the animals. It is as though they were playing a game of "statues" and someone told them to freeze. They don't seem interested in attacking one another. There are no raised paws or bared teeth. They are peaceful and contented with one another and with their environment.

Look at the foreground, the part of the painting that appears closest to you. Why do you think Pippin placed children on his holy mountain?

The children are doing more than just petting a favorite animal. They are showing that it is possible to live together with those who seem different. Pippin suffered from the wars and prejudices of his times. He looked to the children of the next generation to produce a better world.

Why do you think the man in the white robe is in the center of the painting?

He is a shepherd who devotes his life to caring for his gentle flock. We know he is a shepherd because he holds a long stick with a curved top called a shepherd's crook. A shepherd is often used as a symbol of peace. By putting him in the center, Pippin leaves no doubt that peace is the main message of the painting. It is possible that the shepherd is a self portrait of the artist.

Can you find any objects in the background of this landscape that refer to the artist's experiences as a soldier in World War I?

Between the trees of the forest are two ghost-like soldiers on the right. Pippin also included what may be the shadowy image of a tank and T-shaped grave markers. They are his memories of people who suffered in the war. Pippin did not want them to be forgotten.

What gives the painting balance?

The shepherd is just about in the middle of the painting. The figures of the boys and animals placed on either side balance each other. This balanced composition helps the artist achieve a quiet and peaceful setting for his landscape.

How did Pippin use the color red?

The repeated red flowers in the landscape form a pattern that leads our eyes through the painting. Pippin often used red as an accent color in his paintings.

Why do you think the painting carries the date August 9, 1945?

That was the date when the United States dropped an atomic bomb on Nagasaki, Japan, during World War II. Pippin may have felt that during the atomic age there is more need than ever to find a way to live with one another in peace.

Pippin had seen the work of a Pennsylvania artist named Edward Hicks, who had painted a series called *The Peaceable Kingdom* almost 100 years earlier. What do these works have in common?

Try to find a reproduction of *The Peaceable Kingdom* in the school or local library and have students compare it to *Holy Mountain III*.

TELL IT ON THE MOUNTAIN

GOAL:

To create a mixed-media collage (a picture made by pasting paper or other materials on a surface) expressing the theme of peace, which inspired Horace Pippin.

by Billie Jean Walker—6th Grade

WHAT YOU'LL NEED:

- Poster paints
- Brushes
- Scissors
- All-purpose glue
- Heavy white paper
- Markers or crayons
- Two jars of water
- Magazines with pictures of landscapes, mountains, animals, etc.
- Assorted scraps from fabrics and papers such as gift wrap and wallpaper

(Optional: a Polaroid or regular photo of each student—to be cut out and included in the collage. Ideally, the photo will show the student full-length. If you need to preserve the photo, you can make a photocopy of it.)

GETTING READY:

Horace Pippin started a fourth Holy Mountain painting but never finished it. However, until the day he died, he never lost the hope that the entire world would be at peace. What might Pippin have included in Holy Mountain IV?

1. Ask students how they think a perfect world would look. Encourage them to imagine a magical mountain where nothing bad ever happens, a special place where all living things have learned to live happily with one another, a place with no wars or violence, no sickness, hunger, or loneliness. There is only laughter and friendship. Tell students that when they get all their thoughts together they are going to make a collage picturing their own personal Holy Mountain or Peace Mountain.

2. Pippin used a shepherd as the symbol for peace on his holy mountain. Other artists have used flowers, doves, rainbows, hearts, or children holding hands to symbolize peace. Ask each student to decide on a symbol for his or her collage.

3. Some people believe that the shepherd is actually a self-portrait of the artist. If you have pictures of the students, guide the class in cutting out the pictures to incorporate in their collages. If photos are not available, give students the option of drawing self-portraits.

4. Give students time to look through magazines and to cut out objects or words that they think might come in handy for their collages about peace. Suggest that in addition to objects students cut out colors or shapes. If, for example, a student intends to make an apple tree, he or she might save colored magazine pages that use red, green, and brown, and later cut them into appropriate shapes and sizes. Also explain that it is perfectly all right to use parts of an object or a word in a collage.

LET'S BEGIN:

1. Explain that students should start by thinking about the season of the year and the time of day or night they want to show in their collage about peace. How much of the mountain do they wish to show? Like Pippin, they might want a mountain plateau. Perhaps they will design their mountains to show the sloping side or the peak. Whatever students decide, advise them to make the mountain large enough so that they have room to paste their paper cutouts on its surface.

2. They can outline and color their mountains with paint, crayons, or markers.

3. Next, direct students to put in the background. It can suggest day or night. It can show sky or only trees, a combination of the two, or any other perfectly peaceful setting that they can imagine. Caution students not to add much detail. Their cutouts will provide the detail.

4. Wait for the painting to dry.

5. Next, ask students to take out the cuttings they collected and to begin to arrange them on their papers.

6. Once again, alert the students to the red accent that forms a pattern in the Pippin painting. Students can use the patterned scraps of fabric, gift wrap, and wallpaper to achieve a repeated pattern within their own paintings.

7. Demonstrate for students how to put cut-out shapes one on top of the other. This is called overlapping and can add depth and interest to their work.

8. Before students actually start pasting, they should look at the way they have arranged their cutouts on the paper and ask themselves if the arrangement expresses their feelings and ideas. Allow them time to change the placement of cutouts before pasting them down.

9. When students begin pasting, make sure they glue around the back edge of each shape.

10. It is often hard to know when to stop work on a collage. It is a good idea to take time to stand back and look at a work in progress every so often to check that it doesn't look too crowded or too sparse. When students decide to stop, they should put away their materials, sit back, and feel proud of completing a very difficult project.

Vincent Van Gogh

1853 – 1890

Vincent Van Gogh's troubled life began in Holland. His earliest paintings portrayed the lives of poor farmers and coal miners. The colors he used were dull and dark. Later, when he moved to Paris and met the Impressionist artists, he began to use their slashing brush strokes and clear, bright colors.

When it became too cold to paint outdoors, Van Gogh left Paris and moved to the south of France. The brilliant sun and beautiful countryside inspired him to paint without stopping. Even when the sun went down, he continued to paint by sticking candles in the brim of his hat.

Van Gogh invited his friend, the artist Paul Gaugin, to visit him. At first, they painted together, but their friendship was marked by terrible arguments. And when Gaugin decided to leave, Van Gogh was so upset he cut off part of his ear. After that, Van Gogh had to be admitted to the hospital. As his wound was healing, he painted his self-portrait by looking in the mirror. The face he painted shows his pain and sadness.

One after another, he produced some of his most famous canvases, including *The Starry Night*. Even though he often felt depressed and lonely, he rarely allowed himself to rest. Near the end of his life, he painted seventy paintings in seventy days!

Although Van Gogh produced about 800 paintings, only one was sold during his lifetime. Yet his original style continues to influence many artists, and brings joy to millions of people like you.

THE STARRY NIGHT

ARTIST:
Vincent Van Gogh

SIZE:
2'5" x 3'

MEDIUM:
Oil on canvas

DATE:
1889

Most of us have had the experience of looking up in wonder at the night sky.

What moves in Vincent Van Gogh's sky?

Everything seems to be in motion. The rings that form halos around the moon and the stars seem to make them come alive. Paint forms great sweeping spirals of wind that swirl through the sky. They almost looks like waves rushing to the shore.

Which way is the wind moving? Let your hand describe the path of the wind.

Hand gestures can show rolling, swooping, spiraling motions.

What vertical objects did Van Gogh place in the landscape to keep our eyes from moving too quickly across the canvas?

The mysterious flame shape on the left is most probably one of the cypress trees that Van Gogh loved to paint. The church steeple also acts as a stop sign and keeps our eyes from rushing across the horizontal sky.

Where do you think the artist was standing when he saw this scene?

He was probably on a hill. Nobody is quite sure whether this painting represents an actual scene or is the result of Van Gogh's very active imagination. The village in the foreground may be one of the Dutch villages that Van Gogh remembered from his past.

How can you tell that there are people living in the village?

The lights in the houses show that the village is occupied.

What did Van Gogh place in the background?

The starry night sky, which takes up more than half the surface of the painting, is the only thing in the background.

What is in the middle ground?

The middle ground consists of the small area of mountains that divide the sky from the village.

If you could touch the painting, do you think it would feel rough or smooth?

Van Gogh was one of the first artists to use texture to make his paintings look so rich and rough.

How do you think he was able to do this?

Sometimes Van Gogh applied his paint with a knife. Other times he put it on so thickly with his brush that it was raised from the surface. There were times he squeezed tubes of paint directly onto the canvas, and he layered colors one on top of the other. The result is a surface with a texture so rough and bumpy that some of the shapes seem to leap off the canvas. The technique of using thick layers of paint is called "impasto."

Does this painting show reality or fantasy?

It shows both. It is possible to recognize mountains, trees, bushes, and houses. The moon and the stars are placed in the sky where they belong. However, the color and the revolving shapes and forms are so fantastic that they could never be found in nature in exactly that way.

Compare the paintings of Jackson Pollock and Vincent Van Gogh. Can you discover any similarities?

They both let their feelings guide them as they painted. They both used enormous energy as they applied their paint to the canvas, and both became totally involved in the act of creating a picture.

EMOTION IN MOTION

GOAL:

To create a textured landscape in the style of Van Gogh

by Rachel Hirshfeld—2nd Grade

WHAT YOU'LL NEED:

- White oaktag
- Poster paints
- Flour
- Plastic spoons and forks
- Shiny white shelving paper
- Newspaper
- Damp rags
- Two jars of water
- Paper towels

GETTING READY:

1. Finger painting allows the artist a great deal of freedom and is one way to add texture to a painting.

2. First instruct students to put on smocks and line their work surfaces with newspaper.

3. To start this practice session, direct students to place white shelving paper on the newspaper. Direct them to wet their fingers and then to dip them in the color they want to use first.

4. Advise students to work with one color at first, and to experiment by gradually adding a second color. If they mix too many colors together, the paints will lose their freshness and clarity.

5. If the paint is too thick, you or your students can thin it with additional water. If the paint is too thin, you or your students can thicken it with a small amount of flour.

6. Help students understand that their fingers are their brushes. They can use all their fingers at once to make a streaky effect, or they can use just an index finger to shape a more definite line. They can dab the paint on with knuckles or thumbs. Encourage students to invent different textures by using different parts of their hands.

7. Moving quickly, students might want to scrape various designs and textures into the paint with a plastic fork or spoon.

8. They should use the paper towels to blot any excess paint, and they should clean their fingers and tools with a damp rag when they change from one color to another.

9. When the students feel comfortable using finger paints, it is time to go on to the next step.

LET'S BEGIN:

1. Direct students to place fresh newspaper on their work surfaces and to put a piece of oaktag on top.

2. Suggest that students think of an outside scene—either a real or an imaginary landscape. What will the weather be? Is something moving through the air? Is it night or day? Are there mountains or valleys? Are there lakes or waterfalls?

3. Advise students that the sky is a good place to begin and that, like Van Gogh, they should let the sky take up at least half the painting. Encourage students to put some movement in the sky. Now is the time to dip fingers in a color and start.

4. Remind students not to mix together too many colors at once and to keep cleaning their hands with a damp rag.

5. By looking back at their experiments using plastic utensils or different parts of the hand, students can get ideas for adding some contrasting textures to their landscapes.

6. It is a good idea to allow the background sky to dry before students work on the foreground and the middle ground.

8. Van Gogh did not want to imitate nature. He experimented with color and rearranged and reshaped forms. Students, too, should let imagination and energy guide their hands as they move around the paper. Finally, encourage students to step back and admire the results of their flying fingers.

Tao-Chi

1642 – 1707

Over 300 years ago in China, there lived a boy named Chu Jo-Chi. His family was rich and important because they were related to the emperor. But when Chu Jo-Chi was only fourteen years old, a new government came to power and threw out the old emperor and his supporters. Chu Jo-Chi had to run away in order to escape death.

Fortunately, he was hidden by a group of religious men, called monks. For his protection, he changed his name to Tao-Chi, which means "the path of nature."

The monks taught the young man to appreciate the beauty in the world around him. He began to write poetry and paint pictures of trees, rocks, birds, and flowers. For hours he would sit on the floor with his paper on a low table before him. Using a bamboo brush and ink, he created nature paintings of great beauty.

Tao-Chi was different from other artists of his time. He was an independent person who didn't want to copy the art of the past. Instead, he experimented by painting places and objects from his own memory. Often he tried new painting styles. Sometimes his paintings were filled with thick, black, swirling lines. Other times, his lines were thin and delicate.

Tao-Chi has long been recognized as one of China's finest artists. Today, his works are admired by art lovers all over the world.

BAMBOO IN WIND AND RAIN

ARTIST:
Tao-Chi
SIZE:
11′1″ x 3′1 1/4″
MEDIUM:
Ink on paper
DATE:
circa 1695

The Chinese have long considered the combination of calligraphy (artistic writing), poetry, and painting as the highest expression of art.

A favorite subject for many Chinese artists was the drawing of bamboo. Can you guess why this plant was so admired?

The tough bamboo plant may bend, but it never breaks. Even the strongest wind or the hardest rain will not destroy it. It remains fresh and green even during the cold season, and it always grows. It also has many practical uses. It is not surprising that many people look at the bamboo plant as an example for their own lives. The artist Tao-Chi had many difficulties in his life. Like the bamboo, he always had the strength to overcome his troubles and never broke under stress and strain.

How does Tao-Chi suggest that the plant has been battered by wind and rain?

The branches gently curve before the force of the wind, and the heavy rain seems to weigh down the leaves.

Why do you think the artist painted the bamboo leaves in light and dark tones?

The leaves that were painted in lighter tones seem to recede. The darker leaves come forward. The contrast gives the painting depth and movement.

Do you think that Tao-Chi sketched the bamboo before he painted it with ink?

Tao-Chi believed that nature was his teacher. He thought that a good artist should know his subject so well that he could paint it quickly from memory. He probably spent many hours actually observing the growth of the plant. It was only when he felt that he completely understood bamboo that he could go into his studio and create his picture.

How does this painting show the entire life cycle of the bamboo plant?

To the left are the beginning sprouts of a new, young plant. In the middle are the low-growing stalks and leaves of well-established bamboo. On the right, the tall stalks of a mature plant tower over the rest. This is the way all living things grow—in stages from infancy to maturity.

How does the artist balance the tall group of bamboo on the right?

The calligraphy on the left balances the bamboo. The writing is a copy of a well-known old Chinese poem. The Chinese write from right to left and from top to bottom. Since the Chinese language does not have an alphabet, every word is written as a separate sign, or character. Just as every person's handwriting is different, so does calligraphy vary. A good calligrapher will spend years learning to make each character look as beautiful as possible.

Here is a translation of the poem that Tao-Chi copied onto his painting:

"He dallies amid bamboo in the morning, stays in the company of bamboo in the evening; he drinks and eats amid the bamboo, and rests and sleeps in the shade of bamboo. Having observed all the different aspects of the bamboo, he exhausts all the bamboo's many transformations. . . ."

Why do you think Tao-Chi used this particular poem for his scroll, or wall hanging?

It is an expression of the overall importance of bamboo in a person's life.

Can you find the artist's seal in the corner?

Many artists used a seal to sign their work. These seals were usually printed in red ink. Some paintings might have many seals as later owners or admirers placed their own names on the work.

THINK INK!

The rain is falling
The wind is blowing the trees
Nature is hiding

GOAL:

To create a brush-and-ink painting in the style of Tao-Chi

WHAT YOU'LL NEED:

- India ink or black poster paint
- Drawing paper approximately 18" by 5 1/2"
- Brushes
- Black markers
- Red ink pad
- Hole puncher
- Yarn or ribbon to hang scrolls
- Paper toweling
- Newspaper
- 4 small paper cups for each student
- 1" square of Styrofoam for each student
- Patterned wallpaper or gift wrap (optional)
- Glue (optional)

by Eddie Mihalczo—2nd Grade

Note: If you are using an indelible India ink, make sure students protect their clothing with smocks. Alternatively, use a washable black ink.

GETTING READY:

1. More than 1400 years ago, artists in China began to paint with a brush made of bamboo and animal hair. Their ink was not liquid. It was made of burned wood mixed with fish glue. The mixture was pressed into a small rectangle called an ink stick. Since we cannot make our own ink sticks, explain that we will substitute either India ink or black poster paint.

2. Any medium-sized brush that comes to a point can take the place of a bamboo brush. (Optional: You may use brushes of varying thicknesses.)

3. Instruct students to cover their desks or tables with newspapers, which will absorb any excess water, and to place their practice paper on top of the newspaper.

4. Give each student four empty cups to line up on their desks. They will fill the first cup with water—to rinse the brush.

5. Tao-Chi used several variations of black in his painting. Students are now going to create three shades of black: To get the darkest shade, students will use the ink or paint as it comes from the bottle, pouring a small amount into the second cup.

clear water   dark   medium   light

6. Then they will put a little clear water (less than an inch) in both the third and fourth cups. Demonstrate carefully by adding enough ink to each cup to get a very light shade in one and a medium shade in the other.

7. Students should use their brushes to test each of their shades on practice paper. Do the shades contrast enough? If students want to darken a shade, they can just add a little more black; if they want to lighten a shade, they can add a little water. Allow students to keep testing their dark, medium, and light shades until they are pleased with the results.

8. Now encourage students to practice a variety of brush strokes; making thick and thin lines, pushing the brush along the paper, pulling the brush along, making different size dots and dashes, and pressing hard on the brush or twirling it.

9. Instruct students to blot up any excess water or ink with paper toweling.

LET'S BEGIN:

1. When their work surfaces are lined with clean dry newspaper, students should place on top fresh scroll paper in a vertical position.

2. Invite students to select a subject from nature: a tree, a mountain, a waterfall, a flower, or any other outdoor scene that inspires them.

3. Advise students to keep their painting simple, allowing a part of the white background to show rather than trying to paint the entire surface of the scroll.

4. As during practice, students should vary their brush strokes by making some lines wavy and others straight, some lines thick and others thin. They can refer to their practice paper to recall possibilities.

5. In addition, students can vary the shades, making some objects and lines darker than others. Objects in the distance can be a lighter shade than those in the foreground. Overlapping—placing a darker shade over a lighter one—can make a painting look as if it has depth.

6. While the ink is drying, give students time to write a poem or a few brief sentences that describe the scrolls they have created. Then ask them to transfer the poems onto their scrolls, using a thin black marker. Remind students that calligraphy is as important to a Chinese artist as the painting itself.

7. Help students cut small squares (1″ x 1″) out of Styrofoam. These will become seals.

8. Students can make a design of their initials or create a personal symbol for their seals by pressing the point of a pen into the Styrofoam to form the design. Make students aware that whatever they draw into the Styrofoam will be reversed when it is printed.

9. To print the seal, students will first press the Styrofoam onto the red ink pad and then press it on a corner of the scroll. They may have to press hard so that all the ink is transferred to the paper. On the scroll, the seal will appear as a red square with the design showing as the white space within.

10. (Optional) Show students how to glue strips of wallpaper or wrapping paper around the edges of the scrolls to form borders.

11. So that students can hang their scrolls, ask them to punch holes on both sides near the top and to fasten yarn or ribbon through the holes.

Sonia Delaunay

1885 - 1979

Sonia Delaunay was born in Russia, and she moved to Paris in 1905. It was wonderful and exciting to be an artist in the early years of the twentieth century. There was a feeling that change was in the air. Sonia Delaunay and her artist husband, Robert, were fascinated by advances in science and technology. Like other artists of the time, they began to question the traditions of the past. Why should an artist paint only what is real and recognizable?

They believed a new century deserved a new kind of art. Their paintings made no effort to represent persons, places, or animals of the real world. Instead, they worked only with color and shape in a revolutionary style called Abstract Art.

Although she continued to paint through her life, Delaunay also designed many objects for everyday use. Perhaps it was the long, gray winters of her Russian childhood that made her want to surround herself with color. When her first child was born, she pieced together a blanket for him, and combined yards of brightly colored cloth and fur into an exciting arrangement of shapes. She then designed unique fabrics and persuaded the fashion-conscious women of Paris to wear dresses cut from them. Her clothes were a huge success.

She turned her talents to creating other unusual designs for modern life, even decorating a car. Her enthusiasm for experiment led her to try her hand at designing stage sets and costumes for the ballet and theater.

Delaunay felt that she was taking modern art out of the artist's studio. She was one of the first to bring art directly to the people through clothes and furnishings.

ELECTRICAL PRISMS

ARTIST:
Sonia Delaunay

SIZE:
8′2″ x 8′2″

MEDIUM:
Oil on canvas

DATE:
1914

Sonia Delaunay loved color for its own sake.

We sometimes take color for granted. But what if there were no color in the world? How would you feel if the sky, grass, flowers, and trees were all shades of gray?

We surround ourselves with color in our daily lives. We choose certain clothes because their color appeals to us. We paint a room in a particular color because that color makes us feel comfortable. Some colors have the power to make us sad, and others can make us happy. Delaunay's paintings are novel arrangements of dazzling colors.

This painting is called *Electrical Prisms*. What is a prism?

A prism is a crystal. When sunlight passes through a prism, it breaks up into bands of different colors. A raindrop can also act as a prism. The rainbow that is formed in the sky after a rain shower is actually sunlight passing through raindrops. Delaunay spent many hours holding up a prism to the moon and the sun to study how it separates beams of light into different colors. If there is a prism in your school, you might want to duplicate these experiments.

What colors can you see through a prism?

All the colors of the rainbow—violet, indigo, blue, green, yellow, orange, and red. These are the colors in this painting.

Can you guess why the artist also included the word *electrical* in her title?

About the time that she began this painting, electric lights began to replace gaslights on

the streets of Paris. Their glow seemed to form many-colored circular rings against the night sky. The lights delighted Delaunay. She believed that the invention of electricity was one of the marvels of the modern world.

What shape is represented over and over again in this painting?

Circles, semicircles, and arcs (parts of circles) overlap and seem to dance over and under one another.

How does the artist make your eyes move from one circle or arc to an other?

Ribbons of color link the circles.

Try staring at the center of any one of the circles. What happens?

The circle seems to spin in space. Part of the excitement of this work is discovering color in motion.

Did you notice that there are no recognizable people, places, or animals in the painting?

Delaunay did not paint only what she saw with her own eyes. Her paintings are abstract designs of her imagination.

Can you find the writing to the left above the artist's name?

The year before she painted *Electrical Prisms*, Delaunay illustrated a book of poems by her friend Blaise Cendras. She honored him by including his name in her design.

CIRCLES IN THE SQUARE

GOAL:

To create a colorful geometric design in the style of Sonia Delaunay

WHAT YOU'LL NEED:

- Practice paper
- Brushes
- White paper plates
- Rulers
- Compass (optional)
- Newspaper
- Heavy white paper cut into 10″ squares
- Jars of water
- Poster paint—red, yellow, blue, black, and white
- Paper cups for paint
- Plastic plates for mixing colors

by Joseph Nicolosi—5th Grade

GETTING READY:

1. Making a color wheel will help students learn more about color. A color wheel shows how all the colors of the rainbow relate to one another.

2. By placing a ruler appropriately on a white paper plate and drawing a line, students can divide the plate in half. Students can then divide the plate into six equal parts as shown in Diagram A.

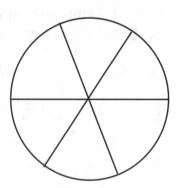

Diagram A

3. Explain that there are three primary colors—red, yellow, and blue—and that all other colors can be made by mixing these three. Give students paper cups with small amounts of red, yellow, and blue paint. Ask students to paint the top center segment of their wheel red. Next, ask them to paint one space blue and one space yellow based on Diagram B. Insist that students clean their brushes thoroughly as they go from one color to the next.

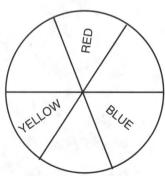

Diagram B

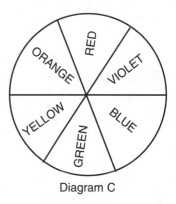

Diagram C

4. Students will now fill in the three empty spaces on the color wheel with the secondary colors, made by mixing together equal amounts of two primary colors. (Mix secondary colors on the plastic plates.) Red + yellow = orange; red + blue = violet; blue + yellow = green. Use Diagram C as a guide to placing secondary colors.

5. Encourage students to figure out what happens if they mix a primary color with the secondary color next to it on the wheel. Students can experiment by mixing yellow and orange or blue and violet on a piece of practice paper. These blends are called intermediary colors. It is always fun to discover new color possibilities.

6. Ask students to notice that each color on the wheel has an opposite. For example, red is opposite green, yellow is opposite violet, and blue is opposite from orange. These pairs of colors are called complementary colors. Complementary colors seem to have the greatest amount of contrast. Ask students which pairs they can find in *Electrical Prisms*.

7. Another way of getting color contrast is to place warm colors such as yellow, orange, and red next to cool colors such as green, blue, and violet. Point out that warm colors are on one half of the color wheel and cool colors on the other. Where in *Electrical Prisms* does Delaunay place warm and cool colors side by side?

LET'S BEGIN:

1. Ask students to think of a Ferris wheel, merry-go-round, helicopter propellers, a pinwheel, or any other circular moving object.

2. Explain that on their square white paper they are going to create a painting using circles, semicircles, and arcs. To draw circles, students may want to use a compass or circular objects, such as paper cups, as a guide. Their goal is to design an interesting overall pattern allowing some of the circles and arcs to overlap one another.

3. Now students are ready to paint their circular designs. Make sure work surfaces are protected with newspaper. Remind students that although they will have only the three primary colors, they should be able to mix a very wide variety of colors.

4. Advise students to place complementary colors next to each other as Delaunay did in *Electrical Prisms*. The same goes for warm and cool colors. Such combinations will add excitement and contrast to students' paintings.

5. Suggest that everyone stay with their first choice of color for a while, using it over again in several of the circles and arcs throughout the drawing. By repeating the same color, the student will unify the design —and will have to wash the brush thoroughly only when changing to a new color.

6. (Optional) If students wish to darken a color, they can add a little black paint. If students wish to lighten a color, they can add a little white paint.

7. Tell students not to worry about drips or accidents. When the paint is dry, they can always change a color. Students should take the time to step back and see if colors look good together.

8. In *Electrical Prisms*, Delaunay painted in the name of her friend, the poet Blaise Cendras. Ask students to think about artists, writers, dancers, or poets they admire. They can include those names in their paintings.

9. Students should sign their paintings and think of exciting titles.

Henri Matisse

1869 – 1954

Henri Matisse was born in the north of France. When he was twenty years old, he became ill with appendicitis. To cheer him up while he was recovering, his mother gave him a box of paints. The colors were so exciting to Matisse that they changed his entire life. For the next sixty years, Matisse used bright colors and simple lines to create a startling new kind of art.

Matisse went to art school in Paris. He studied and respected the great artists of the past, but Matisse didn't want to repeat their styles. He was searching for something different. His friends showed him paintings by a new artist, Vincent Van Gogh. Soon Matisse was experimenting with vivid colors and flickering dots of paint.

He went to the seaside, where he boldly painted blue and orange fishing boats in shocking pink seas. When he painted with the colors he imagined, Matisse's art exploded with feeling. His paintings were so dazzling and powerful that people said they seemed to be filled with wild beasts. Matisse became a leader of a group of artists called *The Fauves*, which means "wild beasts."

Matisse's art became famous throughout the world. Matisse made sculptures, designed books, and even created the wall decorations and stained-glass windows for a chapel.

As Matisse grew old and sick, he continued to work from his bed. Sometimes he attached charcoal to a fishing pole to make his drawings on the wall. Propped up on pillows, Matisse used his scissors to cut out the shapes of swimmers, parakeets and flowers from brilliantly painted paper. The joy of creating stayed with him all his life.

BEASTS OF THE SEA

ARTIST:
Henri Matisse

SIZE:
9'7" x 5'5/8"

MEDIUM:
Collage

DATE:
1950

les bêtes de la mer...
H. matisse 50

Water was special to Matisse. He often lived near the sea and liked to paint its ever-changing beauty.

Pretend you are a fish swimming under the water. All the other creatures of the sea pass before your eyes. Describe what you might see.

You might see a spiny lobster swimming through the waving seaweed, the rapid motion of a snorkeler's flippers, or a slithering eel.

Look at Matisse's *Beasts of the Sea*. Which of his shapes remind you of objects you might find in nature?

Some of the objects look like sea creatures. Some resemble plants.

Look at the shapes Matisse repeats in *Beasts of the Sea*. Are the repeated shapes all the same size? Are they the same color?

By contrasting the size and color of his repeated shapes, Matisse has made the picture more exciting.

***Beasts of the Sea* is a collage, a picture made by pasting paper or other materials onto a surface. Matisse has divided his collage into two columns. How did he keep the two columns from looking as though they would topple over?**

They are balanced like children's building blocks with the larger shapes below and the smaller on top. The collage would not feel as balanced if Matisse had turned the columns upside down.

Would the collage be as interesting if both columns were identical?

Probably not.

Both columns are constructed of several layers of geometric shapes. Can you find the bottom layer?

It is the first layer that Matisse pasted onto the white background. You can find the squares, rectangles, and one triangle that act as a backdrop for all the organic and free-form shapes that Matisse pasted on top.

How many white, curving shapes can you discover? Can you guess why Matisse included them in his collage?

The five white shapes form holes, or "windows." They seem to add light and an open feeling to the design—as though sunlight were filtering through the water.

How did Matisse balance these white shapes?

Black is the opposite of white, and Matisse placed a contrasting black shape near each white shape.

Do you think there are more warm colors or more cool colors in an underwater environment?

The warm colors are yellow, red, and pink while cool colors are blue and green. When we think of a river or the sea we usually think of many shades of blue and green. These "water" colors, which Matisse used over and over again, contrast with the warm-colored shapes.

How did Matisse add movement to the collage?

Curving lines appear to move more than straight lines. Some of the shapes in *Beasts of the Sea* seem to float upward and move in and out of the design. Some shapes extend into the white page. They seem to open up the picture.

How did Matisse add depth to the collage?

By overlapping—pasting one object on top of another—he suggests that the shapes are three dimensional.

DRAWING WITH SCISSORS

GOAL:
To create a collage of an underwater scene in the style of Matisse

WHAT YOU'LL NEED:
- Colored construction paper (several sheets for each child)
- White and black construction paper
- Pieces of white oaktag (12" x 18")
- Scissors
- Glue

by Lauren Katz—4th Grade

GETTING READY:
Matisse created his paper cutouts by trial and error. He would change the positions of his shapes and add new ones until the overall design pleased him. Now, it's your students' turn to experiment.

1. Color changes according to its background. Direct students to cut out two circles of the same color, and to place one circle on a white piece of construction paper, the other on a black piece of construction paper. Elicit comparisons and contrasts. The circle on the light background seems to be the darker of the two. The circle on the dark background seems to be the brighter. The bright circle seems to push forward, and the dark circle seems to recede. Make sure students save their two colored circles.

2. Some colors such as blue, green, and violet are cool colors. Others, like red, yellow, and orange are warm colors. These statements do not mean that some colors have more heat than others. What they do mean is that colors can affect our mood. Tell students to place one sheet of a cool-colored construction paper on top of a warm-colored sheet. Holding the two sheets together, they should cut out several different shapes and place the warm shapes on a white background. What words do the students use to describe how these colors make them feel?

3. Then have students do the same with the cool colors. What words do students use to describe how cool colors make them feel? Which pleases them more? Why? Emphasize that color preference is very personal. Make sure students save their "warm" and "cool" shapes.

4. Varying shapes makes a picture interesting. Direct students to cut out some geometric shapes (squares, rectangles, triangles) and some free-form shapes. Some of the shapes can be pointy, some can contain a hole in the middle, and some can include rough edges. Some shapes can be large and others small. Students should place the shapes on a white background without letting any of the shapes touch one another. Point out that the large shapes seem to be closer than the small shapes.

LET'S BEGIN:

1. Like Matisse, your students may wish to use the cut out rectangles, triangles, and squares to build up two columns that will act as background for their underwater scene. They may choose either warm colors or cool colors or a combination of the two.

2. They may use the shapes they have already cut or cut out new shapes as needed. When they are satisfied with their background arrangement, they should paste it down on the oaktag, making sure to glue around the back edge of each shape.

3. Students are now ready to start the second layer. Remind them to think of all the things real or imaginary that live in the sea.

4. Using scissors and construction paper, students can begin inventing shapes that they want to see in their underwater pictures. Their shapes can be as simple as a round sand dollar, as wiggly as a water snake, or as graceful as moving seaweed. If they create a particularly pleasing shape, encourage them to repeat it in a variety of colors or sizes. They can use the shapes they have already cut out in earlier experiments.

5. After cutting out shapes, direct them to arrange and rearrange the shapes until they find a design they like. Ask students to slowly change the space around their shapes by moving them up and down and then closer together, letting them touch. Kids can also put some shapes on top of other shapes—overlapping them—to produce a feeling of depth. Again, tell students to save thses shapes.

6. When students are satisfied with their arrangements, they should paste down all their cutouts and congratulate themselves on a job well done.